RACING SPORTS

NASCAR RACING

BY HEATHER ROOK BYLENGA

WWW.APEXEDITIONS.COM

Apex is distributed by North Star Editions:
sales@northstareditions.com | 888-417-0195

Produced for Apex by Red Line Editorial.

Photographs ©: Terry Renna/AP Images, cover; Shutterstock Images, 1, 14–15, 20–21, 22–23, 26; Mark Humphrey/AP Images, 4–5; Russell LaBounty/NKP/KINRN/AP Images, 6–7; David Graham/AP Images, 8–9; James P. Kerlin/AP Images, 10–11; AP Images, 12–13; Marc Sanchez/Icon Sportswire/AP Images, 16–17, 29; Logan Whitton/NKP/KINRN/AP Images, 18; Glenn Smith/AP Images, 19; Kevin Abele/Icon Sportswire/AP Images, 24–25; Mel Evans/AP Images, 27

Library of Congress Control Number: 2023900129

ISBN
978-1-63738-539-5 (hardcover)
978-1-63738-593-7 (paperback)
978-1-63738-699-6 (ebook pdf)
978-1-63738-647-7 (hosted ebook)

Printed in the United States of America
Mankato, MN
082023

NOTE TO PARENTS AND EDUCATORS

Apex books are designed to build literacy skills in striving readers. Exciting, high-interest content attracts and holds readers' attention. The text is carefully leveled to allow students to achieve success quickly. Additional features, such as bolded glossary words for difficult terms, help build comprehension.

TABLE OF CONTENTS

CHAPTER 1

RACE DAY

Forty NASCAR drivers wait for a sign. The **grand marshal** shouts, “Drivers, start your engines!” Forty engines roar to life.

Before each race, NASCAR drivers go a short distance to warm up their tires and brakes.

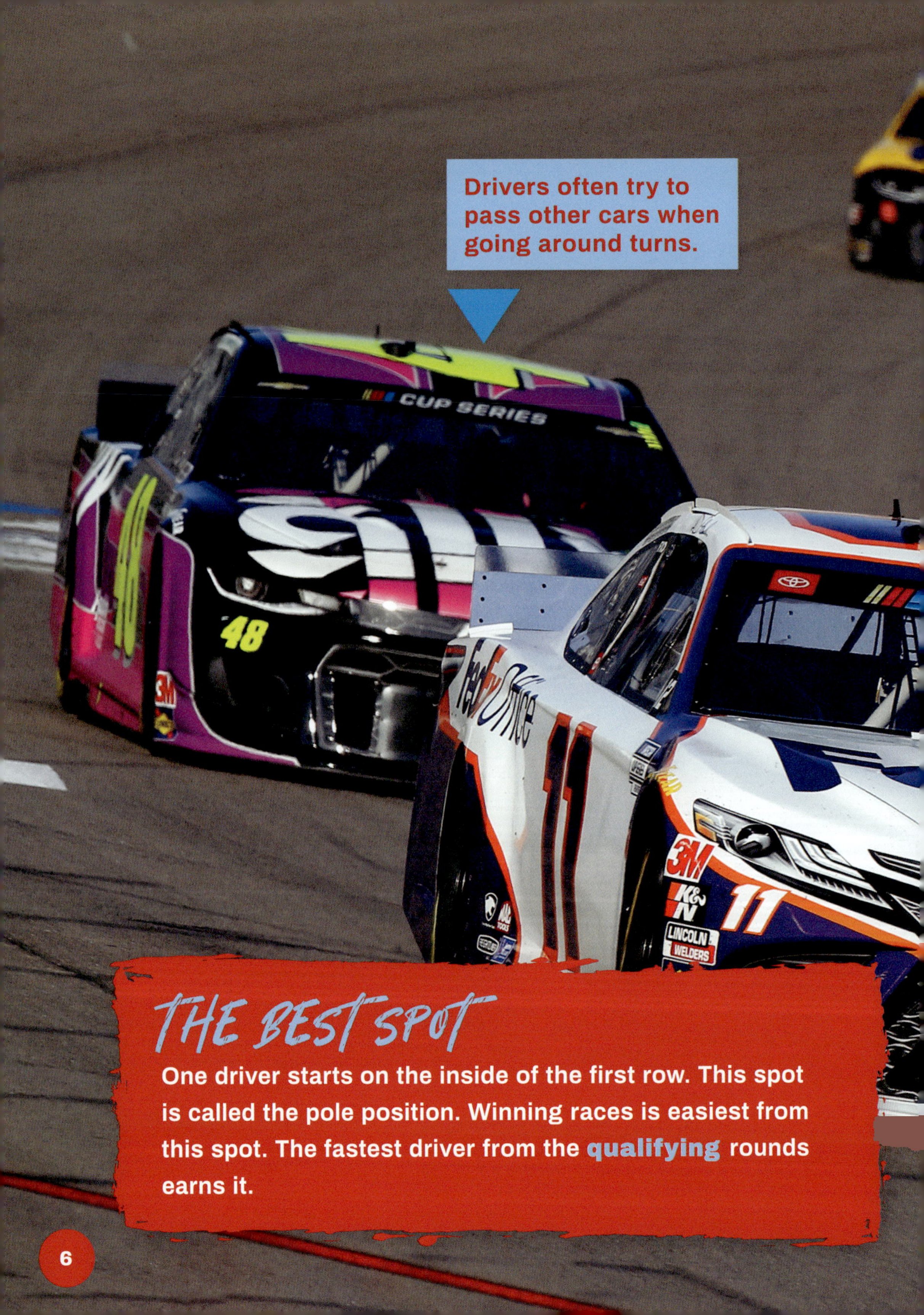

Drivers often try to pass other cars when going around turns.

THE BEST SPOT

One driver starts on the inside of the first row. This spot is called the pole position. Winning races is easiest from this spot. The fastest driver from the **qualifying** rounds earns it.

The green flag waves, and the race begins. The drivers take off. They zip around corners and zoom down **straightaways**.

A checkered flag tells drivers the race is over.

By the last lap, two cars are very close. One driver noses ahead. He crosses the finish line, and the checkered flag waves!

FAST FACT

Most NASCAR races are between 400 and 500 miles (644–805 km) long.

CHAPTER 2

NASCAR History

Car racing became popular in the early 1900s. Some people raced **stock cars** on beaches, dirt tracks, and city streets. There were no set rules. Every race was different.

Early stock cars were much slower than cars today. They went less than 70 miles per hour (113 km/h).

Then, in 1947, a group of drivers met. They created the National Association for Stock Car Auto Racing (NASCAR). This group planned a series of races.

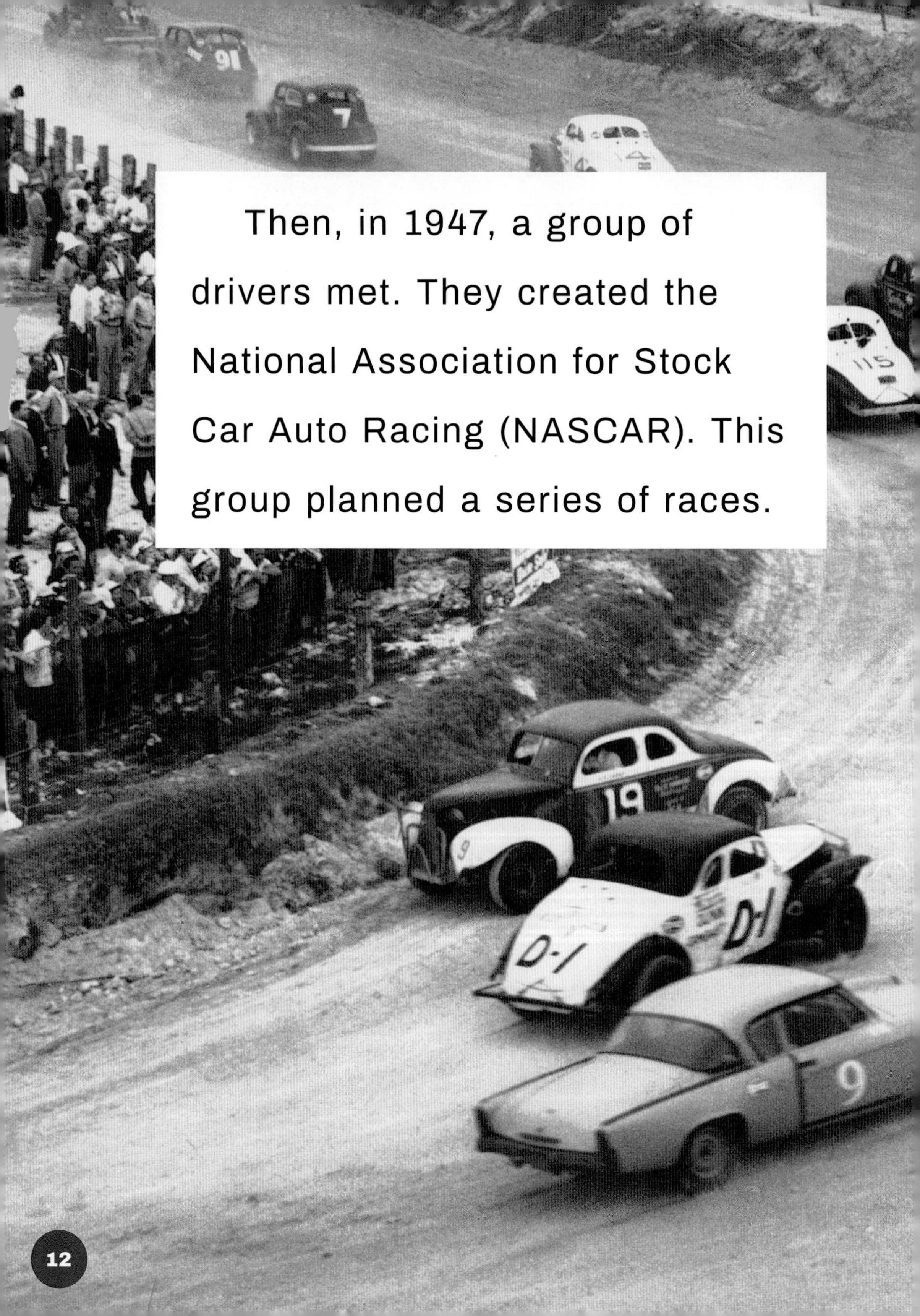

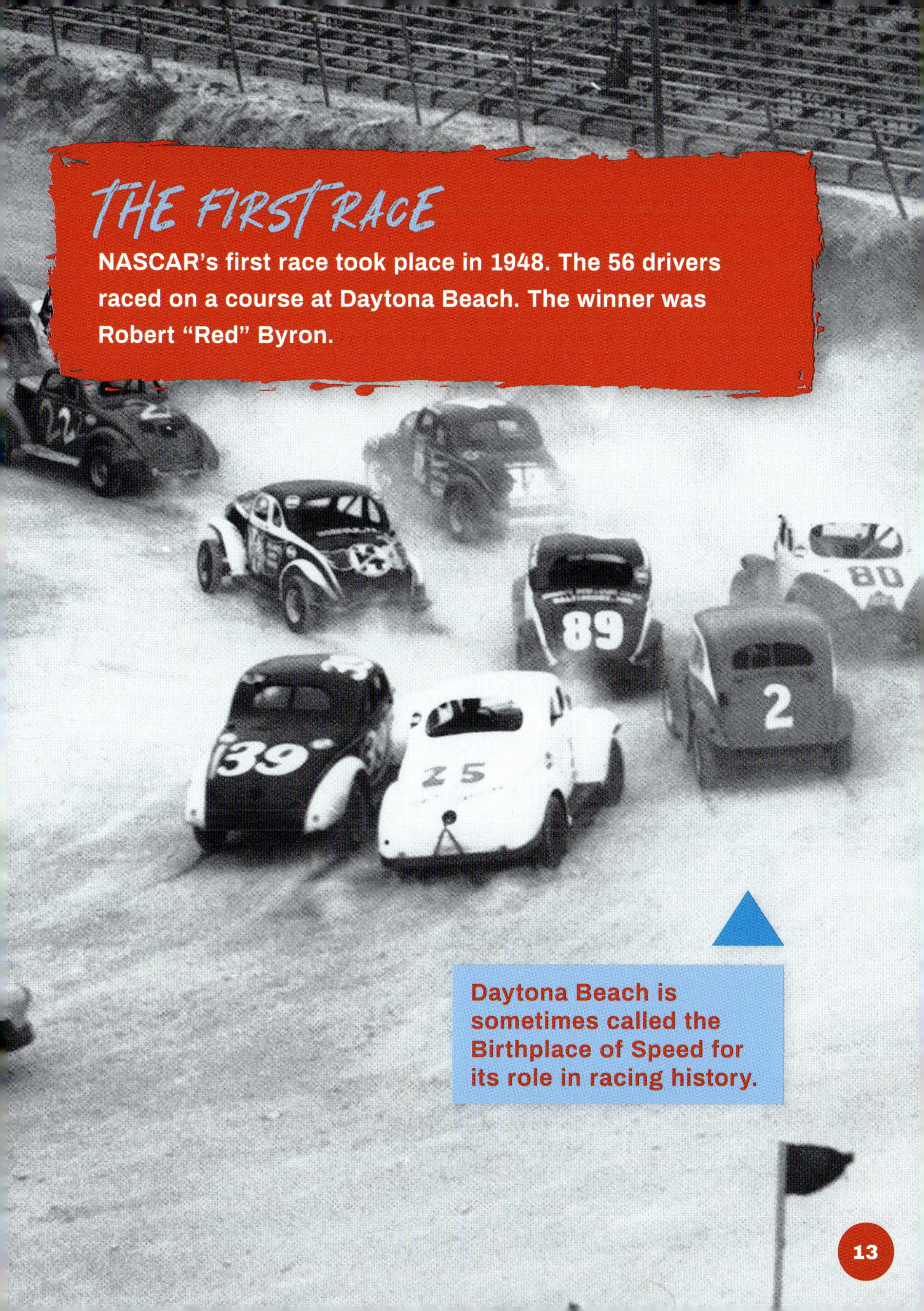

THE FIRST RACE

NASCAR's first race took place in 1948. The 56 drivers raced on a course at Daytona Beach. The winner was Robert "Red" Byron.

Daytona Beach is sometimes called the Birthplace of Speed for its role in racing history.

Over time, the cars got faster. NASCAR added more races, too. The first Daytona 500 took place in 1959. By the 1980s, NASCAR had many fans.

The Bristol Motor Speedway is a famous NASCAR site. It can hold more than 150,000 people.

FAST FACT

The Daytona 500 is the first race in every NASCAR season.

CHAPTER 3

RACES AND TRACKS

Every NASCAR season has 26 regular races. Drivers get points for high finishes. The top 16 drivers advance to the **playoffs**.

Drivers can get points for high finishes and for leading some parts of races.

There are 10 races in the playoffs. In each race, drivers are **eliminated**. By the final race, only four drivers are left. The fastest one wins the Drivers' Championship.

Jimmie Johnson has won the Drivers' Championship seven times.

DRAFTING

Drafting helps drivers gain speed. To draft, one car follows closely behind another. The front car blocks the wind so the back car can go faster with less work.

When drafting, cars may be just a few inches apart.

NASCAR races can use several kinds of tracks. Many tracks are short ovals. Superspeedways are longer ovals. Road courses add more types of turns.

The Talladega Superspeedway is NASCAR's biggest oval track.

FAST FACT

NASCAR drivers belong to teams. Each team can race up to four cars.

CHAPTER 4

THE NEED FOR SPEED

NASCAR race cars are made for speed. Their powerful engines help them go more than 200 miles per hour (322 km/h).

Every NASCAR race car weighs at least 3,300 pounds (1,497 kg).

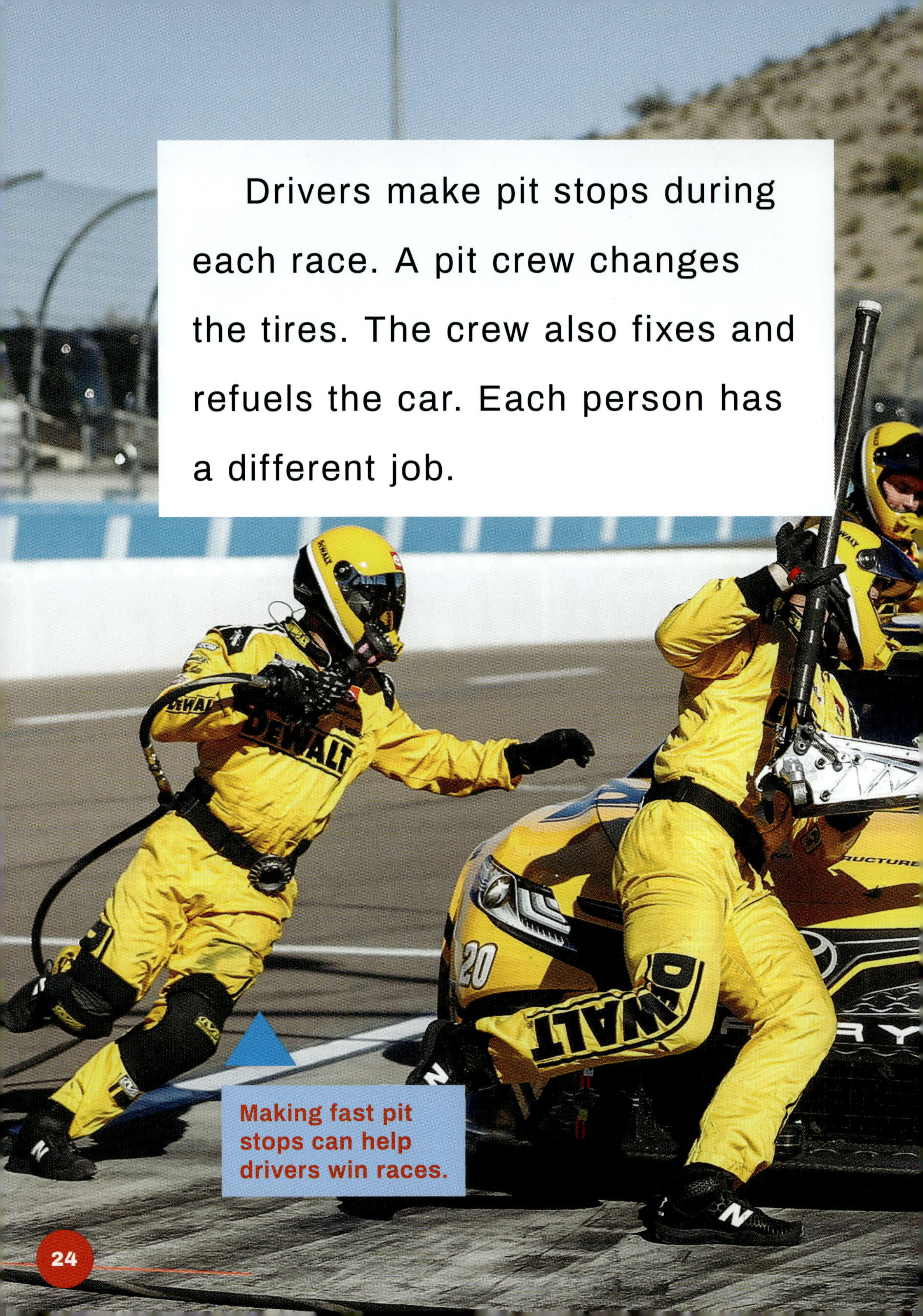

Drivers make pit stops during each race. A pit crew changes the tires. The crew also fixes and refuels the car. Each person has a different job.

Making fast pit stops can help drivers win races.

FAST FACT

The fastest recorded NASCAR pit stop was only 8.6 seconds long.

Sometimes cars catch fire during races.

NASCAR races can be dangerous. So, cars have safety features. Strong steel **frames** and foam bumpers **protect** drivers if they crash. Drivers wear helmets, too.

FLAGS

NASCAR races use flags to send messages to drivers. Green means "go." Yellow tells drivers to be careful. A white flag means it is the last lap. A checkered flag waves for the winner.

A yellow flag might wave if there is a crash or something on the track. Drivers slow down until the track is clear.

COMPREHENSION QUESTIONS

Write your answers on a separate piece of paper.

1. Write a few sentences explaining the main ideas of Chapter 2.

2. Would you like to watch a NASCAR race? Why or why not?

3. What kind of NASCAR tracks have many types of turns?

    A. road courses
    B. short ovals
    C. superspeedways

4. What is one reason NASCAR races are dangerous?

    A. Drivers wear lots of safety equipment.
    B. The high speeds put drivers at risk.
    C. The racetracks are very bumpy.

5. What does **advance** mean in this book?

*Drivers get points for high finishes. The top 16 drivers **advance** to the playoffs.*

- **A.** lose a race
- **B.** quit driving
- **C.** move ahead

6. What does **features** mean in this book?

*So, cars have safety **features**. Strong steel frames and foam bumpers protect drivers if they crash.*

- **A.** parts of cars
- **B.** ways of moving
- **C.** extra drivers

Answer key on page 32.

GLOSSARY

eliminated

Removed from an event or contest.

frames

The metal parts that give race cars their shape.

grand marshal

A person chosen to lead the events on race days.

playoffs

A set of races after the regular season to decide the champion.

protect

To keep safe.

qualifying

Types of earlier races used to pick where drivers will start in later races.

stock cars

Types of race cars that have the frames of regular cars but have other parts changed or added for racing.

straightaways

The parts of racetracks that are straight.

TO LEARN MORE

BOOKS

Adamson, Thomas K. *Stock Cars*. Minneapolis: Bellwether Media, 2019.

Clayton, Annette M. *The Daytona 500*. Mendota Heights, MN: Apex Editions, 2023.

Fishman, Jon M. *Cool Stock Cars*. Minneapolis: Lerner Publications, 2019.

ONLINE RESOURCES

Visit **www.apexeditions.com** to find links and resources related to this title.

ABOUT THE AUTHOR

Heather Rook Bylenga lives in the Pacific Northwest with her family. Outdoors, she can be found hiking or running. Indoors, she can be found curled up on her couch with a book and a cup of tea.

INDEX

ANSWER KEY:

1. Answers will vary; 2. Answers will vary; 3. A; 4. B; 5. C; 6. A